LINCOLN

ENCYCLOPEDIA of PRESIDENTS

Abraham Lincoln

Sixteenth President of the United States

By Jim Hargrove

Consultant: Charles Abele, Ph.D.
Social Studies Instructor
Chicago Public School System

CHILDRENS PRESS ®

CHICAGO

Abraham Lincoln,
sixteenth president
of the United States
(photograph taken
by Mathew Brady on
February 9, 1864)

Library of Congress Cataloging-in-Publication Data

Hargrove, Jim.
    Abraham Lincoln / by Jim Hargrove.
        p.   cm. — (Encyclopedia of presidents)
    Includes index.
    Summary: Traces the life of the frontier clerk, storekeeper,
lawyer, politician, and Civil War President.
    ISBN 0-516-01359-9
    1.   Lincoln, Abraham, 1809-1865 — Juvenile
literature.   2.   Presidents — United States — Biography —
Juvenile literature.   [1.   Lincoln, Abraham, 1809-
1865.   2.   Presidents.]   I. Title.   II. Series.
E457.905.H29   1988
973.7'092'4 — dc19   88-12296
[B]   CIP
[92]   AC

Picture Acknowledgments

AP/Wide World Photos — 5, 6, 8, 17, 23, 26, 40,
42, 47, 54, 59, 60, 63, 64, 66, 70, 71, 73, 75, 76,
79 (bottom), 83

The Bettmann Archive — 24, 28, 41, 44, 68, 80,
88

Historical Pictures Service, Chicago — 14, 30, 35,
39 (2 pictures), 55, 57, 87 (bottom)

Library of Congress — 4, 13, 62, 84

The National Archives/U.S. Signal Corps — 12

The National Archives/U.S. War Department
General Staff — 50

The National Park Service — 61

North Wind Picture Archives — 33, 87 (top)

Photri, Inc. — 65, 82 (2 pictures), 89

U.S. Bureau of Printing and Engraving — 2

Vision Quest — 56, 74, 79 (top)

Cover design and illustration
by Steven Gaston Dobson

Abraham Lincoln,
Mary Todd Lincoln,
and their sons
Thomas ("Tad," left)
and Robert Todd

Table of Contents

Chapter 1

Freedom's Hour

Early in the afternoon of September 22, 1862, President Abraham Lincoln sat at the head of a wooden table in the White House. For a time, he talked with the seven members of his cabinet. Lincoln, dressed in a dark suit, dark vest, and tie, said that a popular speaker of the day named Artemus Ward had sent him a book with a funny chapter. The president read the chapter out loud, and some of the cabinet members laughed at the funny passages. But most wondered how Lincoln could read jokes at such a tragic time.

The United States was in the midst of a civil war, the bloodiest war ever fought on American soil. Angered by the efforts of some people to outlaw slavery, eleven southern states were trying to break away from the United States and form a new nation, the Confederate States of America. War had broken out between Confederate and Union soldiers in April 1861.

Scene after the Battle of Antietam, by Union combat artist Captain James Hope

As Lincoln continued to read the funny chapter to his cabinet, a number of people in the room must have thought about a gruesome Civil War battle that had been fought just five days earlier. Shortly before the battle, about 50,000 Confederate soldiers led by General Robert E. Lee had crossed the Potomac River to invade the northern states. On September 17, the soldiers encountered a Union army of about 70,000 men at Antietam Creek, near the town of Sharpsburg, Maryland. In the Battle of Antietam that followed, nearly 5,000 soldiers died and more than 20,000 more were wounded or recorded as missing. Although the casualties on both sides were about the same, Lee retreated southward the following day. The battle was considered a victory for the North, but the price of winning had been terrible.

President Lincoln continued reading the chapter from the book by Artemus Ward. In the silly story, the author brought some wax figures of the disciples of Jesus to the town of Utica, New York. There, some of the townspeople reacted to the figures as if they were real. The president laughed out loud at the silly situations, but some of the cabinet members remained silent.

"Gentlemen," the president said as he looked at the blank stares of his advisers, "why don't you laugh? With the fearful strain that is upon me night and day, if I did not laugh I should die, and you need this medicine as much as I do." Cabinet member Salmon P. Chase noted that the president then began to look more serious. "Gentlemen," he said, "I have, as you are aware, thought a great deal about the relation of this war to Slavery. . . ."

Lincoln went on to explain that he had decided to issue an executive order freeing the slaves in all the states rebelling against the United States, if the armies of those states did not stop fighting by New Year's Day, 1863. He called his order a Proclamation of Emancipation, which became better known as the preliminary Emancipation Proclamation. The president had read an early draft of the proclamation to the cabinet some months earlier. Now he read the final draft, which included these words:

"That on the first day of January in the year of our Lord one thousand eight hundred and sixty-three, all persons held as slaves within any state, or designated part of a state, the people whereof shall then be in rebellion against the United States shall be then, thenceforward, and forever free. . . ."

Although a number of American presidents had been strongly opposed to slavery, none before Lincoln had dared to declare it illegal. Many people, including the majority of the justices on the U.S. Supreme Court, felt that only the individual states had the power to declare slavery legal or illegal within their boundaries. But now the United States was at war with itself, involved in an enormous civil war. Lincoln felt he could use his wartime powers to issue the Emancipation Proclamation.

At the time, nearly four million Negro slaves were held in the United States—the majority, though not all of them, inside states that had joined the Confederate rebellion. Although Lincoln felt strongly that slavery was morally wrong, his reasons for issuing the Emancipation Proclamation were complex. In a letter to newspaper editor Horace Greeley, he wrote: "My paramount object in this struggle is to save the Union, and is not either to save or to destroy slavery. If I could save the Union without freeing any slave I would do it, and if I could save it by freeing all the slaves I would do it; and if I could save it by freeing some and leaving others alone I would also do that." Lincoln closed his letter by adding the following: "I have here stated my purpose according to my view of official duty; and I intend no modification of my oft-expressed personal wish that all men every where could be free."

Lincoln was making it clear that keeping the United States whole was his most important consideration. There were advantages, however, in threatening to free the slaves. Freed slaves would be allowed to join the Union Army to fight against Confederate soldiers. Also, the act might keep some European nations, such as Great Britain, from officially recognizing and perhaps aiding the Confederate States of America. Finally, Lincoln knew that it was simply the right thing to do, that it would destroy the root cause of the Southern rebellion.

The preliminary Emancipation Proclamation, the document Lincoln signed in September 1862, gave the Southern states a hundred days to put down their arms. If they had done so, the end of slavery would surely have been delayed. But the Civil War raged on. On New Year's Eve, at the end of 1862, many groups of black Americans gathered in candle-lit rooms to await midnight. That was freedom's hour, the time slaves were to be set free in the Confederate states. Blacks around the nation waited up the long evening to welcome the joyous moment in.

At noon on January 1, 1863, the final version of the Emancipation Proclamation was brought to President Lincoln. As he signed it, he said, "If my name ever goes into history, it will be for this act, and my whole soul is in it."

At the time President Lincoln signed it, the final Emancipation Proclamation gave real freedom only to some of the nation's slaves. Although slavery was practiced in Delaware, Maryland, Kentucky, Missouri, and a portion of western Virginia, these areas had refused to join the rebelling Confederacy. Lincoln did not use his powers to outlaw slavery in those loyal states. It was the eleven Confederate States of America that no longer recognized the power of the president of the United States. The Union Army would be able to enforce the Emancipation Proclamation only in the American South.

Abraham Lincoln reads the Emancipation Proclamation to his cabinet.

Suddenly there was a great new purpose for many of the Union soldiers fighting the war. Every time the Union Army advanced deeper into the South, more and more slaves would be freed. Thousands chose to run for their lives toward the battle lines to the north. Before the end of the Civil War, nearly 200,000 former slaves joined the Union Army to fight Confederate soldiers. Without them, the Union might not have won the Civil War.

Still, freedom from slavery for all Americans was not guaranteed until the Thirteenth Amendment to the Constitution was ratified near the end of 1865—after Abraham Lincoln was dead. But at the stroke of midnight, at the instant when the year 1862 became 1863, slavery in America was dealt a crushing blow. More than anyone else, certainly more than any other American president, Abraham Lincoln ended slavery in America.

"Master Lincoln is everywhere," a former slave said about the sixteenth president. "He walks around this world like the Lord."

PROCLAMATION OF EMANCIPATION

BY THE PRESIDENT OF THE UNITED STATES OF AMERICA.

Whereas, On the Twenty-Second day of September, in the year of our Lord One Thousand Eight Hundred and Sixty-Two, a Proclamation was issued by the President of the United States, containing, among other things, the following, to wit:

"That on the First day of January, in the year of our Lord One Thousand Eight Hundred and Sixty-Three, all persons held as Slaves within any State, or designated part of a State, the people whereof shall then be in rebellion against the United States, shall be then, thenceforth, and **FOREVER FREE**, and the *Executive Government of the United States,* including the Military and Naval Authorities thereof, *will recognise and maintain the freedom of such persons,* and will do no act or acts to repress such persons, or any of them, in any efforts they may make for their actual freedom.

"That the Executive will, on the First day of January aforesaid, by proclamation, designate the States and parts of States, if any, in which the people thereof respectively shall then be in rebellion against the United States, and the fact that any State, or the people thereof, shall on that day be in good faith represented in the Congress of the United States by members chosen thereto at elections wherein a majority of the qualified voters of such State shall have participated, shall, in the absence of strong countervailing testimony, be deemed conclusive evidence that such State and the people thereof are not then in rebellion against the United States."

Now, therefore, I, ABRAHAM LINCOLN, PRESIDENT OF THE UNITED STATES, by virtue of the power in me vested as **Commander-in-Chief of the Army and Navy of the United States** in time of actual armed rebellion against the authority and government of the United States, and as a fit and necessary war measure for suppressing said rebellion, do, on this First day of January, in the year of our Lord One Thousand Eight Hundred and Sixty-Three, and in accordance with my purpose so to do, publicly proclaim for the full period of one hundred days from the day of the first above-mentioned order, and designate, as the States and parts of States wherein the people thereof respectively are this day in rebellion against the United States, the following, to wit: — Arkansas, Texas, Louisiana, (except the Parishes of St. Bernard, Plaquemines, Jefferson, St. John, St. Charles, St. James, Ascension, Assumption, Terre Bonne, La Fourche, St. Mary, St. Martin, and Orleans, including the City of Orleans,) **Mississippi, Alabama, Florida, Georgia, South Carolina, North Carolina, and Virginia,** (except the forty-eight counties designated as West Virginia, and also the counties of Berkeley, Accomac, Northampton, Elizabeth City, York, Princess Ann, and Norfolk, including the cities of Norfolk and Portsmouth,) and which excepted parts are for the present left precisely as if this Proclamation were not issued.

And by virtue of the power and for the purpose aforesaid, I do order and declare that **ALL PERSONS HELD AS SLAVES** within said designated States and parts of States ARE, AND HENCEFORWARD **SHALL BE FREE!** and that the Executive Government of the United States, including the Military and Naval Authorities thereof, will recognize and maintain the freedom of said persons.

And I hereby enjoin upon the people so declared to be free to abstain from all violence, UNLESS IN NECESSARY SELF-DEFENCE; and I recommend to them that in all cases, when allowed, they LABOR FAITHFULLY FOR REASONABLE WAGES.

And I further declare and make known that such persons of suitable condition will be received into the armed service of the United States, to garrison forts, positions, stations, and other places, and to man vessels of all sorts in said service.

And upon this act, sincerely believed to be AN ACT OF JUSTICE, warranted by the Constitution, upon military necessity, I invoke the considerate judgment of mankind and the gracious favor of ALMIGHTY GOD!

In Testimony Whereof, I have hereunto set my name, and caused the seal of the United States to be affixed.

Done at the CITY OF WASHINGTON, this First day of January, in the Year of our Lord One Thousand Eight Hundred and Sixty-Three, and of the Independence of the United States the Eighty Seventh.

[L. S.]

By the President,

William H. Seward
Secretary of State.

A. Lincoln.

J. MAYER & Co LITH. 4 STATE ST. BOSTON.

Chapter 2

Young Abraham

In 1776, the year the United States declared itself independent from England, there was a captain in the Virginia militia named Abraham Lincoln. He was the grandfather of the Abraham Lincoln who became sixteenth president of the United States. Soon after the end of the American Revolution, Grandfather Lincoln decided to follow his good friend Daniel Boone through the Cumberland Gap and into the wilderness of Kentucky. With his wife Bathsheba and five children, he settled along Kentucky's Green River in 1782.

About four years later, while Abraham was working in a field near his cabin, a shot rang out from the woods. He fell to the ground. An Indian ran out of the woods and stood over the dying man. Then another shot was heard, and the Indian slumped downward. Mordecai Lincoln, one of Abraham and Bathsheba's three sons, had killed the Indian who had just killed his father.

One of the sons who witnessed the bloody scene was named Thomas Lincoln. Thomas would grow up to become the father of the famous president. In June of 1806, in the little settlement called Elizabethtown, Thomas Lincoln married a young woman named Nancy Hanks. She was also known as Nancy Sparrow, because she had been adopted by a family named Sparrow. The Lincoln's first child, Sarah, was born in 1807.

For a short time, the Lincolns lived on the farm of George Brownfield, where Tom did carpentry work and helped with the farming. Soon, Tom built a one-room log cabin along a creek near the town of Hodgenville, a little more than ten miles from Elizabethtown. The cabin was typical for poor farmers in the Kentucky frontier. It had a door that swung open on leather hinges, a single tiny window, and a dirt floor. In this humble cabin, the sixteenth president of the United States was born on Sunday morning, February 12, 1809. Abraham Lincoln was named after his grandfather who had been killed by an Indian more than twenty years earlier.

The same day that Abraham was born, Tom walked about two miles up a dirt path to where the Sparrow family lived. "Nancy's got a baby boy," Tom announced to the Sparrows. Several members of the Sparrow family traveled to the Lincoln cabin to see the little baby. One of them was Abraham's nine-year-old cousin, Dennis Hanks, who, like Nancy Lincoln, had been adopted by the Sparrows. Dennis asked Nancy if he could hold the infant child.

"Be careful, Dennis," the mother warned, "for you are the first boy he's ever seen." Dennis held little Abraham

The log cabin where Abraham Lincoln was born

in his arms, but the baby soon began to cry without letting up. Discouraged, Dennis handed Abraham to his aunt, Betsy Sparrow, who was also visiting.

"Aunt, take him!" Dennis years later remembered saying. "He'll never come to much." But, of course, he did.

Remarkably, the little log cabin where Abraham Lincoln was born nearly two centuries ago still stands today. But now it is inside a huge concrete memorial building with six columns in front and a long concrete staircase leading up to it. It is part of the Abraham Lincoln Birthplace monument in Hodgenville, Kentucky. Much of the wooded, rolling land around the cabin is also reserved for the historic monument.

Just a hundred yards or so from the cabin is Sinking Spring, where the Lincoln family got its drinking water. Today, visitors to the memorial can walk down a short stone staircase to get a close look at the spring itself, where water bubbles up from the rocky ground below. Because of this spring, the Lincolns' farm was called Sinking Spring and, more often, Rock Spring.

Covered by rolling hills, forests, and streams, the land around the Rock Spring farm was a pretty sight. But the soil was filled with rocks and hard clay, making it difficult to farm. When Abraham was just three years old, his family moved to another Kentucky farm, about fifteen miles northeast of his birthplace. The thirty-acre farm, along the dirt road that connected Louisville with Nashville, was called Knob Creek because of a nearby stream.

The young boy saw many travelers moving along the Louisville-Nashville Road. Pioneer families hoping to settle farther west and south came by in their large covered wagons. Peddlers selling household trinkets and questionable medicines traveled on mules, on horseback, and in wagons. Even politicians traveling to the state legislature in Lexington often traveled on the road that passed by the Lincolns' little cabin.

Even for a young child, there were plenty of chores on a farm in the near-wilderness of Kentucky. Wearing only a long shirt, young Abe often rode a horse attached to a plow at planting time. After long trenches were scratched into the earth with the plow, he helped his father plant corn, potatoes, and beans. Throughout the warm months, he pulled out the weeds that grew around the crops.

There were plenty of other chores as well. The youngster cleaned out the ashes of the cabin's fireplace and filled a box with wood that his father had chopped. While his father hunted deer, bear, and smaller animals with a rifle, young Abraham looked for wild nuts and berries growing in the woods and clearings around the farm. In the fall, there was even more work harvesting crops, grinding corn into flour by scraping it between two stones, and, always, gathering firewood for the long winter ahead. It was even possible to work outside when it was dark, by burning knots from pine trees for light.

Near the end of the Lincolns' stay in Kentucky, young Abe briefly attended school. During the winter months of 1815 and 1816, when chores around the farm were relatively light, he and his sister Sarah walked about four miles each way to a log cabin schoolhouse with no windows on the Cumberland Road. The type of school Abraham attended in Kentucky was known as a "blab" school, because the students recited their lessons out loud. At the blab school, Abraham began to learn the alphabet, numbers, and even simple multiplication problems. But he did not attend the school for long. Problems for his family were beginning to mount.

Many Kentucky pioneers were finding their homelands taken away from them because they did not have the right kind of papers to prove that they owned their land. Bit by bit, all of the land of Daniel Boone, the state's most famous pioneer, had been taken away from him. And Thomas Lincoln was sued for trespassing on his own land. Land laws in Kentucky were anything but fair.

An increasing number of wealthy landowners were moving into Kentucky, bringing with them Negro slaves. Before long, more than half the people in Hardin County, where the Knob Creek farm stood, were slaves. For wealthy landowners, slaves made life much easier. But for poor white workers, such as Thomas Lincoln, the large numbers of slaves made jobs hard to find. Few wealthy people would hire poor white men when they could have slaves do the work without pay. Thomas Lincoln was already opposed to slavery on moral grounds. His young son began to realize that slavery could cause problems for white people as well as black people.

In 1816, Thomas and Nancy decided to move to Indiana Territory, where slavery was outlawed. Thomas made a flatboat and loaded it with most of his family's possessions. Leaving the Kentucky farm, he floated down Knob Creek to the Salt River and on to the wide Ohio River. On the Ohio, the boat capsized and most of the Lincolns' furniture and other household goods were lost. But Thomas pushed on, crossing the Ohio and walking northward into Indiana. When he found a suitable area of land, he claimed it by notching some trees with his axe. Thomas would have to pay for the land eventually, at the rate of $1.25 per acre. Then he walked the hundred miles or so back to the Kentucky farm to get his family.

"We removed from Kentucky to what is now Spencer County, Indiana, in my eighth year," Abraham wrote many years later. "This removal was partly on account of slavery; but chiefly on account of the difficulty in land titles in Kentucky."

Abraham was still two months shy of his eighth birthday when he and his family arrived at their new homesite in southern Indiana in December of 1816. That very same month, the Territory of Indiana became a free state of the Union—that is, a state where slavery was outlawed. During the coldest months of the winter the family huddled in a three-sided shelter, warmed only by a campfire. By late February, shortly after Abraham's eighth birthday, the family had completed a log cabin with a dirt floor and a stone fireplace. It must have been a relief to move inside.

In 1817 the Sparrows and Dennis Hanks, now nineteen years old, followed the Lincolns to Indiana and settled nearby in the area known as Little Pigeon Creek. Tragedy struck the following year. Many settlers began suffering from a mysterious disease the frontier people called "milk sickness." Dennis Hanks's adopted parents, Tom and Elizabeth Sparrow, both became sick and died.

Soon after, Abraham's mother Nancy died at the age of thirty-four from the disease. Thomas made a coffin out of cherry wood and buried his wife on a hillside. Dennis Hanks moved in for a time, and Abe's twelve-year-old sister Sarah did her best to sew, cook, and keep house for the three men. The following year, 1819, Abe was kicked in the head by a horse "and apparently killed for a time," as he put it. But Abe recovered and regained that year not only his health but a new mother as well. Thomas traveled back to Kentucky and married a widow named Sarah Bush Johnston. For weeks while Thomas was gone, Abe and Sarah lived in the little cabin. Then one morning four horses and a wagon pulled up to the door.

"Here's your new mammy," Thomas told his children as they rushed outside to greet him. Traveling with the newlyweds were Sarah's three children: John, Sarah, and Matilda. Suddenly the lonesome cabin was filled with people, including three different Sarahs: Abe's sister Sarah, his new stepmother Sarah, and his new stepsister Sarah. The new arrivals also brought many household items with them, including feather mattresses and pillows, wooden furniture, and a variety of kitchen utensils. Abe's new stepmother, whose nickname was Sally, treated her adopted children as well as she treated her own. Abe soon grew to love her deeply.

Pigeon Creek lay in an area of dense forests. In order to farm the land, hundreds and then thousands of trees had to be cut down and cleared. "Though very young," Lincoln wrote as a grown man, "I was large for my age, and had an axe put into my hands at once; and from that till within my twenty-third year, I was almost constantly handling that most useful instrument—less, of course, in plowing and harvesting seasons."

For much of his youth, Abe Lincoln spent his days alone in the forest working with an axe. He cleared acre after acre of land for farming, cut and split firewood, and split logs into rough rails to make fences. Strong, solid fences were important for the frontier farmers, to keep their livestock in. "My how he could chop," a neighbor said of Abe. "His axe would flash and bite into a sugar tree or sycamore, down it would come. If you heard him felling trees in a clearing, you would say there were three men at work, the way the trees fell."

One of many paintings of Abraham Lincoln as a boy

All the wood chopping made Abraham strong and healthy, but he always was unhappy about how he spent his childhood. John Romine, a man for whom Abraham once worked, recalled that his young employee "said to me one day that his father taught him to work, but he never taught him to love it." Although he attended school briefly during the winter in Indiana, Abe's total schooling throughout his life amounted to less than a year.

Lincoln studying by firelight

Despite the fact that he had little time for school, the boy managed to educate himself. Even while he still lived in Kentucky, he began reading books at every opportunity. Although books in the Indiana frontier were scarce, Abraham borrowed and read what few volumes he could find. Among those he read were the Bible, *The Adventures of Robinson Crusoe, Aesop's Fables,* a biography of George Washington, and just about anything else he could get hold of. "A friend is someone who finds me a new book to read," he once said.

Neighbors often saw him in the fields, working behind a plow and reading a book at the same time. Some—including, sometimes, his own father—thought that the young man was lazy to want to read so much. Many simply did not understand. When Dennis Hanks saw his cousin reading *Aesop's Fables*, he said, "Abe, them yarns is all lies." But Lincoln answered, "Mighty darn good lies, Denny."

People throughout the Little Pigeon Creek settlement learned that Abe was skilled at reading and writing. Using ink made from the blackberry plant and a feather pen, Abe wrote letters for many of his neighbors. He also began writing poetry for his own amusement. The earliest known poems by Abraham Lincoln were written in a homemade notebook he used during his brief visits to school:

> Abraham Lincoln
> his hand and pen
> he will be good
> but god knows when

> Abraham Lincoln is my nam[e]
> And with my pen I wrote the same
> I wrote in both hast[e] and speed
> and left it here for fools to read

Abraham continued to write poetry throughout his life, and many of his poems were considerably better than his earliest efforts. In the meantime, he grew into a tall, thin, and very strong young man. By his late teens, he stood about six feet four inches tall. And despite his love of reading, he worked hard in the forests and clearings of southern Indiana.

Early in 1828, Abraham learned the sad news that his only natural sister, Sarah, had died during childbirth a few days before her twenty-first birthday. Young Abe felt a tremendous sense of sadness that lasted for weeks. For the rest of his life, he suffered from occasional attacks of depression.

Abe worked briefly as a helper on an Ohio River ferryboat. In 1828, at the age of nineteen, he helped pilot a flatboat down the Ohio and Mississippi rivers to New Orleans. During the journey, he was attacked by a gang of thieves and had to fight for his life. After fending off the attackers, he and his friend, Allen Gentry, returned to Little Pigeon Creek by steamboat. When he arrived, Abe promptly gave the twenty-five dollars he had earned to his father.

By the time he was twenty years old, Abraham was fascinated by the law. He began attending trials held in the log cabin courthouses in nearby Rockport and Boonville. Wanting to learn more about the law, he managed to borrow and read a copy of the *Revised Statutes of Indiana*. Noting that lawyers often referred to the Declaration of Independence and the Constitution, he studied those documents as well.

Abe's new interests would soon lead him to a career as a lawyer and, eventually, a politician. But he would not start in Indiana, for changes were in store. In March of 1830, Thomas and Sally decided to move once again, this time to Illinois. Illinois would remain Lincoln's home for a quarter of a century, until it was time for him to travel to the White House.

Chapter 3

The Representative
from New Salem

Early in 1830, when Abraham was twenty-one years old, Thomas Lincoln sold his farm and moved his family west to Illinois. Although the future president was now old enough to live on his own, he decided to accompany his family in the move.

"The mode of conveyance was wagons drawn by ox-teams," Lincoln wrote years later. "I drove one of the teams. We reached the county of Macon [Illinois], and stopped there sometime within the same month of March. My father and family settled a new place on the north side of the Sangamon river, at the junction of the timberland and prairie, about ten miles westerly from Decatur. Here we built a log-cabin, into which we removed, and made sufficient rails to fence ten acres of ground, fenced and broke the ground, and raised a crop of sown corn upon it the same year."

A typical flatboat going down the Mississippi River

The Lincolns' first winter in Illinois was a hard one. The entire family fell sick in the fall, and the winter was worse than anyone could recall. By the spring of 1831, Abe was anxious to get out of the cabin and earn some money. He and two other members of his family decided to take another cargo-carrying flatboat down the Sangamon, Illinois, and Mississippi rivers to New Orleans. They talked a local businessman named Denton Offutt into financing the project. Offutt also went along for the ride.

While still on the little Sangamon River, about twenty miles northwest of the Illinois town of Springfield, the flatboat got caught on a dam near the tiny village of New Salem. Abraham thought of a clever way to get the boat loose from the dam, and Denton Offutt was impressed by the young man's resourcefulness.

New Salem, with less than a hundred settlers, was a wild frontier town. Convinced that New Salem was about to become a boom town, Offutt decided to buy a store in the village and hire Abraham Lincoln to work in it. Abraham accepted, completing his voyage to New Orleans and returning to New Salem about three months later.

It didn't take long for Abe to get to know his new neighbors, and the villagers quickly grew to like the tall young man. Lincoln seemed to enjoy the company of some of New Salem's rowdier citizens. Although he spent some free time with them, joined in their wild storytelling, and even liked to wrestle and roughhouse, he never joined them in drinking alcohol.

Abe was at an age to consider marrying, but since his early teens he had felt shy and awkward around girls and women his own age. About one relationship he once said, "Others have been made fools of by the girls, but this can never with truth be said of me. I most emphatically, in this instance, made a fool of myself."

There was a single exception. For a time, he lived in a rented room at New Salem's Rutledge Tavern. There he met the owner's nineteen-year-old daughter, Ann Rutledge. Ann and Abe became friends, although it is unlikely that they ever became romantically involved. Ann was engaged to marry another man. But Abraham enjoyed their friendship nevertheless. He also enjoyed the company of Ann's father, the proud owner of thirty books and the organizer of a local debating society. He was greatly saddened when, a few years later in the summer of 1835, Ann became ill and died, probably of typhoid fever.

As he had done in Kentucky and Indiana, Lincoln spent much of his free time reading books and trying to improve his education. He studied public speaking from a book called *Columbian Orator* and the rules of the English language in *Kirkaham's Grammar*. He even continued to study, on his own, mathematics and geometry, subjects he enjoyed throughout his life.

Now well past his twenty-first birthday, Abe was old enough to vote, and he took an interest in politics. He also noted that Denton Offutt's prediction that New Salem would soon become a boom town was wrong. It had already stopped growing; the general store where Abraham worked was doing less and less business. Abe decided that he could help the town, and begin a successful career in politics, if he could figure out a way for larger boats to travel on the little Sangamon River. In 1832, at the age of twenty-three, Lincoln announced that he was a candidate for the Illinois state legislature.

His campaign was interrupted in April, when a rider galloped into town and announced that the Indian chief Black Hawk was on the warpath in northern Illinois. The governor of the state was asking for volunteers to fight the Indians, the rider announced, and Abraham quickly joined a small group of New Salem's young men who headed northward. Lincoln was surprised when his company of soldiers elected him captain.

The Black Hawk War was not one of America's proudest episodes. Most of the Indians, only trying to regain their land that had been illegally sold to whites, were slaughtered. Even women, children, and tiny babies were

Sauk and Fox chief Black Hawk

killed. But Lincoln took no part in the slaughter. He was released from duty before encountering the Indians.

Later in his life, however, he couldn't help making fun of the way many politicians glorified their military careers. In an 1848 speech he recalled his war experience, saying, "I had a good many bloody struggles with the mosquitoes; and although I never fainted from loss of blood, I can truly say I was often very hungry."

He returned to New Salem just two weeks before the scheduled election. Immediately, he began a whirlwind campaign for the state legislature. "Fellow Citizens," he said in one brief speech, "I presume you all know who I am. I am humble Abraham Lincoln. . . . My politics are short and sweet like the old woman's dance. I am in favor of a national bank. I am in favor of the internal improvement system and a high protective tariff. . . . If elected, I shall be thankful; if not, it will be all the same."

His New Salem neighbors did what they could to help Lincoln win the election. They gave him 277 out of 300 votes cast in the New Salem precinct. But other towns were included in the district, and in those places he was not so well known. Lincoln lost his first election. There were four seats available in the legislature, but he ran eighth in a field of thirteen candidates.

His attempt to enter politics foiled, Lincoln needed to find some kind of work. In the late summer of 1832, he bought several stores on credit and became involved in a number of financial deals in New Salem with a partner named William Berry. Unfortunately, Berry spent much of his time sipping whiskey from a barrel in the back of one of the stores. And Lincoln couldn't resist spending most of his time talking politics with his customers and reading law books. Before long, the partnership failed and Lincoln was deeply in debt.

The following year, President Andrew Jackson appointed him postmaster of New Salem. The presidential appointment was a bit of a surprise, because Lincoln was in favor of a national bank system, bitterly opposed by Jackson. Lincoln joked that his new twenty-five-dollar-a-year job was "too insignificant to make his politics an objection."

Lincoln served as New Salem's postmaster until 1836, when the little post office was closed because of New Salem's diminishing population. In the meantime, the post office was located in a general store owned by a man named Sam Hill. There, postmaster Lincoln read the newspapers that came into the store. He soon added to his

Lincoln as New Salem postmaster

tiny salary by working as an assistant surveyor for Sangamon County. But by 1834, he found it impossible to pay off all his debts.

In the court case that followed, a number of his personal possessions were taken away, including his horse and surveying instruments. In January of 1835, his one-time partner William Berry died, and Lincoln had to take on many of his debts as well. The total indebtedness amounted to about $1,100, an amount so high for a man working on a tiny salary that Lincoln began calling it the "National Debt." Like many other poor people, he could simply have left the state, and his debts, behind. Instead, he spent the next fifteen years paying them off.

Despite Lincoln's money problems, there was good news in 1834. He decided to run again for the Illinois legislature. His jobs as postmaster and surveyor often required him to travel around the New Salem countryside. As he did, he shook hands and talked to voters, sometimes even helping them harvest their crops. His honest and helpful campaign paid off. He was easily elected to the legislature in the August election.

In those days the capital of Illinois was Vandalia, a town with just eight hundred permanent residents, about seventy-five miles southeast of Springfield. Lincoln borrowed two hundred dollars to pay off his most urgent debts and paid sixty dollars for a new suit, the most expensive clothing he had ever owned. At 6:00 A.M. on the morning of November 28, 1834, the smartly dressed representative from New Salem boarded a stagecoach in Springfield bound for Vandalia.

When Lincoln arrived in Vandalia, the capital of Illinois was just fifteen years old. The town's muddy public square was surrounded by ramshackle buildings. The statehouse, where the legislature met, was a two-story brick building in such poor repair that it seemed ready to fall apart. Now, however, a new session of the state legislature was about to begin and the town looked its best. Well-dressed politicians and their wives walked up and down the wooden sidewalks. Buggies and wagons moved through the muddy streets, the horses and sometimes the passengers plagued by mosquitoes and flies.

During his first term in the Illinois legislature, Lincoln often followed the advice of a Springfield lawyer named

John Todd Stuart. The two men had met while Lincoln was campaigning and quickly became friends. Stuart was beginning his second term as a legislator. Both Lincoln and Stuart believed in the loosely defined policies of the Whigs, a new political party that was organized in 1834, the same year that Lincoln was elected. Actually, Whig politicians believed in many different policies, but virtually all opposed the Democratic party of President Andrew Jackson.

During the winter of 1834 and 1835, Lincoln and the other Illinois representatives met in the first floor of the statehouse. A wood-burning stove and a fireplace heated the large room. Candles provided light on cloudy days and during the evening. While pieces of plaster sometimes fell from the ceiling, the representatives considered and voted on more than a hundred issues, from building bridges to appointing government workers. Most of the time, Lincoln voted the same way as his friend John Todd Stuart and the other Whigs. The Whigs soon discovered that the twenty-five-year-old politician was an expert writer. They often asked him to help write bills they hoped would become new laws.

With the encouragement of John Stuart, Lincoln continued to study law by reading books, many of them borrowed from Stuart. "I studied with nobody," Lincoln wrote. "I still mixed in the surveying to pay board and clothing bills. When the Legislature met, the law books were dropped, but were then taken up again at the end of the session. I was re-elected in 1836, 1838, and 1840. I was not a candidate afterwards."

During the years Lincoln served in the Illinois legislature, the nationwide debate over the issue of slavery was becoming more intense. In the cities of the northeast, people called abolitionists were demanding an end to slavery throughout the country. Frightened by the growing protests of the abolitionists, a number of southern state legislatures voted to ask northern state legislators to condemn the activities of the abolitionists.

Most members of the Illinois legislature agreed with the southerners. In January of 1837, by a vote of 77 to 6, the House of Representatives condemned the abolitionists and agreed that individual states had the constitutional right to permit slavery. Lincoln was one of only six Illinois representatives to vote against the measure.

Although he knew that human slavery was immoral, Lincoln was worried by the abolitionists who were trying to stop it. Late in February of 1837, Lincoln and Daniel Stone, another Whig legislator, presented the other state politicians with a written complaint about the recent vote. "The institution of slavery is founded on both injustice and bad policy," the men argued. But they also agreed with their coworkers that the abolitionists were dangerous. They believed that the protests against slavery would soon result in violence.

Lincoln's concerns were proved correct in a matter of months. Elijah Lovejoy, the publisher of an abolitionist newspaper in Alton, Illinois, was murdered by an angry mob opposed to his beliefs. Not content with murder, the mob also burned his office and dumped his printing press into the Mississippi River.

Abolitionist Elijah P. Lovejoy (right) was murdered by a crazed, proslavery mob in Alton, Illinois, in 1836. The mob also destroyed his offices (below).

Lincoln, the young lawyer, in a Springfield courtroom

Slavery was becoming the most important issue of the day. But while he served in the Illinois legislature, Lincoln had other, more personal concerns. He continued studying the law by borrowing and reading books from John Stuart's library. By 1836 he was already writing wills and deeds for his neighbors. Later the same year, he successfully completed an examination before the justices of the Illinois supreme court. In March of 1837, the clerk of the supreme court entered his name on the official list of lawyers allowed to practice in Illinois.

The street in downtown Springfield where Lincoln and William Herndon had their law office

Until this time, Lincoln returned at the end of each legislative session to his home in New Salem. But now that, at the age of twenty-eight, he had become a lawyer as well as a politician, he decided to move to nearby Springfield. That very same year, the capital of Illinois was moved from Vandalia to Springfield. There, in an office at 4 Hoffman's Row, above the Springfield circuit court room, he opened an office with his new partner and old friend, John Todd Stuart.

Chapter 4

Springfield

When Lincoln arrived in Springfield at the end of 1837, about 1,500 people lived in the town. He was already respected in his new home because he had campaigned hard to make Springfield the new capital of Illinois. Although the residents of the town were honored to be living in a state capital, the town itself was hardly prepared. The first sessions of the Illinois senate, house of representatives, and supreme court were held in three different Springfield churches.

The salary of an Illinois legislator was three dollars a day—by Lincoln's standards, a princely sum. But this salary was paid only during the few months when the legislature was in session. And Lincoln still had many debts to repay. Although he was both a politician and now a lawyer, he was still very poor, unable to afford his own home. Joshua Speed, the owner of a Springfield general store, felt sorry for the lawyer. He let Lincoln live in a room above the store without paying rent. Lincoln and Speed became longtime friends.

William Herndon, Lincoln's friend and law partner

Gradually, the legal firm of John Todd Stuart and Abraham Lincoln developed substantial business, and Lincoln's fortunes began to improve a bit. When Stuart defeated a young Illinois politician named Stephen A. Douglas for a seat in the U.S. House of Representatives in Washington, most of the firm's casework was handled capably by Lincoln himself.

In the spring of 1841, Lincoln carried a few of his papers and other possessions across the street and began a partnership with another lawyer, Stephen T. Logan. Three years later, in 1844, Lincoln entered into his third and final partnership, this time with a younger lawyer named William H. Herndon. But in the meantime, while his professional work was increasing, Lincoln's love life at last took a turn for the better.

In the fall of 1839, twenty-year-old Mary Ann Todd, a relative of John Todd Stuart, came to Springfield for an extended visit with her sister and her sister's husband, Ninian Edwards. Mary was a member of a wealthy family from Lexington, Kentucky. Lincoln had seen the attractive, slightly plump girl around town. He had also heard that she was bright and well educated. Ordinarily, Lincoln never attended dances because he was a poor dancer and felt uneasy in the company of women. However, he decided to attend his first formal dance when he heard that Mary would be there.

At the dance, he finally worked up the courage to speak to her. "Miss Todd, I should like to dance with you the worst way," he said.

"He certainly did," Mary told a friend after the dance was done. But although Lincoln was not much of a dancer, something about him appealed to the young woman from Kentucky. Despite the fact that she had many other suitors, including the well-respected politician and lawyer Stephen A. Douglas, Mary soon fell in love with Abraham. The pair decided to marry on January 1, 1841.

But problems arose almost immediately. Mary's sister and her sister's family felt that Lincoln was a crude, backwoods politician. They didn't feel he was right for a cultured young woman like Mary. They also doubted that Lincoln could earn enough money to support a woman used to luxurious living. When he learned about these objections, Lincoln was crushed. He began to think that Mary's sister and her sister's husband were right. Finally, the marriage was called off.

"If what I feel were equally distributed to the whole human family," Lincoln wrote to John Todd Stuart, "there would not be one cheerful face on the earth." For months, Lincoln fell into a severe depression. His friends and associates in the Illinois legislature noted that he looked sickly and miserable. His friend Joshua Speed, and Joshua's mother, gradually nursed him back to health. By the middle of 1842, he and Mary Todd once again decided to marry, despite the feelings of Mary's relatives. The wedding took place in the Edwards home on November 4, 1842.

For Mary Todd Lincoln, accustomed to large homes and comfortable surroundings, married life took some getting used to. For a year, the Lincolns lived in a rented room at Springfield's Globe Tavern. Abraham sent small amounts of money to his parents and was still paying off his New Salem debts. Mary, on the other hand, was not accustomed to pinching pennies, and she frequently argued with her husband over financial matters. In May of 1844, about nine months after their first son, Robert Todd, was born, the Lincolns managed to buy a two-story house in Springfield.

Between 1843 and 1853, Mary Todd Lincoln gave birth to four sons. Tragically, only the first, Robert Todd, lived a long life. (A statesman and lawyer, Robert died in 1926.) The other three, Edward, William, and Thomas, all died before the age of twenty-one, although Thomas, nicknamed Tad, outlived his famous father. Nevertheless, the death of a child twice saddened the father, already inclined to periods of depression.

Opposite page: Mary Todd Lincoln

Following his fourth term in the Illinois house of representatives in 1840 and 1841, Lincoln did not run again for the Illinois legislature. He turned all of his energies, for the time, to the legal profession. By 1844, around the time he formed a partnership with William Herndon, his work began to require travel. Twice each year, judges traveled to different counties in Illinois's eighth judicial circuit to try cases. Lawyers, Lincoln now among them, frequently traveled with them. Lincoln rightly suspected that he would soon be traveling much farther.

For about three years, a number of Whig politicians had promised to nominate Lincoln to run for the U.S. House of Representatives. On May 2, 1846, a party convention named him as the Whig candidate for the U.S. House of Representatives from the Seventh Illinois Congressional District.

Just eleven days later, the United States declared war on Mexico in a dispute over ownership of Texas and, soon enough, California. Actually, under the direction of President James Polk, American soldiers had been fighting Mexicans for some weeks before war was officially declared. While Lincoln campaigned for the U.S. Congress, troops organized in Springfield and set off for Mexico.

Although Lincoln was well respected in Springfield and the surrounding counties, he had raised some eyebrows by refusing to attend church services. He did, however, attend a religious meeting run by Peter Cartwright. Cartwright was a Methodist preacher who was running against Lincoln as a Democrat in the upcoming election for U.S. congressman.

At one point during the meeting, Cartwright told his audience: "All who desire to lead a new life, to give their hearts to God, and go to Heaven, will stand." A number of people stood up. Then Cartwright added, "All who do not wish to go to hell will stand." Now everyone stood up, except for Abraham Lincoln. Cartwright continued his speech noting that "all of you save one has indicated that you do not wish to go to hell. The sole exception is Mr. Lincoln, who did not respond to either invitation. May I inquire of you, Mr. Lincoln, where are you going?"

"I am going to Congress," Lincoln answered, along with some other remarks. And he was right. By a margin of 6,340 votes to 4,829 for Cartwright, Lincoln won the August election. But it was more than a year until he was scheduled to take his seat in the House of Representatives.

During the long wait, Lincoln finished up his business in Springfield. He also attended, in the summer of 1847, an important convention in Chicago dealing with rivers and harbors. The convention was well attended by delegates from all over the United States. Newspapers as far away as Boston and New York commented favorably on the congressman-elect from Illinois.

A few months later, the Lincolns rented out their Springfield home for ninety dollars a year and prepared for the trip to Washington. On the way, they stayed for three weeks with Mary's family in Lexington, Kentucky. For the first time in many years, Abraham Lincoln was staying in slave country. Near the Todd house, he witnessed a slave auction and saw the unfortunate people who were bought and sold there like cattle.

A "lantern slide" showing Lincoln in the New Orleans slave market

The Lincolns and their two boys arrived in Washington, D.C., on December 2, 1847. Washington was a city of about thirty-four thousand people, including several thousand black slaves. More than a few new politicians, Lincoln among them, were surprised at the condition of the nation's capital. Nestled between elegant government buildings were run-down shacks and buildings of every description. Garbage was strewn along many of the streets. Cows and pigs roamed the alleys. Large groups of slaves, with heavy chains connecting their legs, moved like prisoners in the numerous slave markets. After three months, Mary had seen enough. She took her two boys and moved back to Lexington to stay with her family.

As Lincoln began his term sitting in the back row of the House of Representatives, an American army had just crushed the soldiers of the Mexican government. Soon, a peace treaty would be signed in which Mexico would be forced to sell more than a million square miles of land to the United States. The war, which added much of California, New Mexico, and Texas to the United States, was very popular with many Americans. But Lincoln felt it was wrong.

On December 22, 1847, Lincoln spoke in the House, asking President Polk to explain where Mexican troops had attacked Americans. Lincoln was suggesting that the president could not name such a place, thus proving that American soldiers had really started the war. When the president did not respond, Lincoln again addressed the House of Representatives on January 12, 1848. He again attacked the war, in a stand he later described in writing.

"I thought the act of sending an armed force among the Mexicans was *unnecessary*," he wrote, "inasmuch as Mexico was in no way molesting, or menacing the United States or the people thereof; and that it was *unconstitutional*, because the power of levying war is vested in Congress, and not in the President."

Little more than two weeks after Congressman Lincoln made his speech, a peace treaty signed by Mexican officials arrived in Washington. For the price of fifteen million dollars, Mexico surrendered California, New Mexico, and Texas as far south as the Rio Grande River to the United States. For the first time, American land stretched from the Atlantic to the Pacific Ocean.

Lincoln's stand against what some Whig politicians called "Mr. Polk's war" was unpopular among many Americans, especially Democrats. Democratic politicians and newspapers, even in Illinois, accused him of being disloyal and stupid. For his part, Lincoln objected to the war because it had been started under the direction of President Polk, not by a congressional vote, as required by the Constitution.

In one other major effort, Congressman Lincoln introduced a measure that would free all children born to slaves in Washington, D.C., after January 1, 1850. In this attempt, too, he was unsuccessful. In his two major efforts in the House of Representatives, Lincoln had done his best to stand up for the principles of fairness and freedom. He lost on both counts. One victory came when the Whig presidential candidate, Zachary Taylor, for whom Lincoln campaigned energetically, won the presidential election in 1848.

When he accepted his nomination for congressman, Lincoln had agreed with Illinois Whigs that he would serve only a single two-year term. He agreed to step aside in 1849 and let his former law partner, Stephen Logan, run for his seat.

When his term was over, Lincoln had been led to believe he could expect a good government job. But many politicians were angered by his attacks on President Polk and the Mexican War, and the position was withheld from him. In 1849, at the age of forty, Lincoln returned to Springfield, Illinois, to continue his private law practice with his partner, William Herndon.

The law practice grew substantially as the well-known ex-congressman returned to work. Although he had to repair many damaged feelings brought about by his speeches in Washington, he soon did so. Before long, he was arguing cases before the Illinois supreme court and handling important cases for the Illinois Central Railroad and large business corporations. He also found the time to work for his friends and neighbors, once again establishing his good character in Illinois.

But just as things were returning to normal, tragedy struck. On February 1, 1850, his four-year-old son Eddie died. Mary was shattered. Abraham threw his energies into his work to forget his pain. It gradually faded over the next three years as Mary gave birth to two more sons.

Tragedy was also developing for the United States as a whole. During the decade of the 1850s, arguments over slavery became increasingly bitter and dangerous. As the years passed, one event after another brought the nation ever closer to civil war.

Since 1820, the U.S. government had dealt with the issue of slavery under the terms of a law called the Missouri Compromise. That law made slavery legal only south of the 36°30' line, Missouri's southern border. But the creation of new American states and territories in the West strained the 1820 agreement. Thirty years later, Congress passed a series of laws known as the Compromise of 1850. These laws allowed California to enter the Union as a free state. At the same time, people in the new territories of Utah and New Mexico were allowed to decide for themselves whether to permit slavery.

Stephen Douglas, nicknamed the "Little Giant," was 5'4" tall.

The idea of the voters' control over the practice of slavery gained support in 1854. On January 23 of that year, Stephen A. Douglas, the Democratic senator from Illinois, introduced a bill called the Kansas-Nebraska Act. It allowed people in more new territories, in this case Kansas and Nebraska, to vote on the issue of slavery.

In the Illinois cities of Springfield, Bloomington, and Peoria, Lincoln spoke out against the Kansas-Nebraska Act. He feared that the new law would open up the entire American West to slavery. He also felt that it would increase the tension between those who favored slavery and those who were opposed to it. Other politicians were

Outsiders invading Kansas to sway the slavery vote

opposed to the Kansas-Nebraska Act as well. On March 20, 1854, a number of antislavery Whigs and Democrats met in Ripon, Wisconsin, to form a new political organization, the Republican party. Lincoln joined the Republican party two years later.

Lincoln's fears about the Kansas-Nebraska Act were well-founded. "Bleeding Kansas" became a battleground for the advocates and opponents of slavery. Arguments erupted into gun battles, rigged elections, lynchings by angry mobs, and outright murders.

Major General John C. Frémont

Although his legal practice in Springfield was doing well, Lincoln decided to reenter the political arena. On November 7, 1854, he was elected to the Illinois legislature on a platform opposed to the Kansas-Nebraska Act. But almost immediately, he resigned to make an unsuccessful run for the Senate. The voters of Illinois were not ready to send an antislavery Whig to the U.S. Senate.

Like a number of other Whigs, Lincoln decided to cast his fortunes with the new Republican party. At its 1856 convention, the Republicans nominated John C. Frémont for president. Although the vice-presidential nomination went to William L. Dayton, 110 delegates cast their votes for Lincoln. Lincoln made dozens of speeches for the new Republican party, urging that slavery not be allowed to spread. He also asked people to remain calm, to keep the issue of slavery from splitting the nation apart.

President James Buchanan

Despite Lincoln's efforts, the Republican presidential candidate lost Illinois and, by a narrow margin, the nationwide vote. Democrat James Buchanan won the election. But the Republicans won many other state elections and showed that they were becoming a strong political party.

Two days after President Buchanan was inaugurated, the Supreme Court handed down its famous Dred Scott decision. In that case, the court ruled that black people had no rights that whites had to respect. The court ruled that, contrary to Stephen A. Douglas's Kansas-Nebraska Act, not even state or territorial voters or legislatures could make slavery illegal. Douglas did his best to support the strange ruling, but Lincoln attacked it strongly in a number of public speeches.

On June 16, 1858, Illinois Republicans nominated Lincoln to run against Democrat Stephen Douglas for the U.S. Senate. In his famous acceptance speech, Lincoln attacked the Dred Scott decision and other recent events that made it law that "if any one man chooses to enslave another, no third man shall be allowed to object." He also noted that opposition to slavery anywhere in the nation was becoming increasingly strong in many of the free states.

"In my opinion," he said, "it will not cease, until a crisis shall have been reached, and passed." Quoting from the Bible, he said, " 'A house divided against itself cannot stand.' I believe this government cannot endure, permanently half slave and half free. I do not expect the Union to be dissolved—I do not expect the house to fall—but I do expect it will cease to be divided. It will become all one thing, or all the other."

The speech was printed in newspapers around the country. Many northern papers noted that the contest between Lincoln and Douglas mirrored the problems of a troubled nation. The *New York Times* stated that Illinois was "the most interesting battle ground in the Union."

Lincoln proposed a series of debates between himself and Douglas. At first Douglas refused face-to-face encounters, but under increasing pressure, he finally agreed to a series of seven debates. The Lincoln-Douglas debates, concentrating on the issue of slavery, attracted nationwide attention. The debates were held between August 21 and October 15, 1858. They were festive affairs, although several took place in the rain. Brass bands played, cannons were fired, and large crowds turned out.

Lincoln and Douglas debate during the 1858 campaign for U.S. senator from Illinois.

Douglas argued that he was neither for nor against the spread of slavery. He only wanted the citizens of each state or territory to decide the issue for themselves. He also attacked Lincoln as a friend of the northern abolitionists. According to Douglas, Lincoln would free millions of slaves so that they could take away jobs from white people and marry their daughters.

Douglas's attacks put Lincoln on the defensive. He pointed out that he was against marriages between the races and did not consider blacks fully equal to whites. But he insisted that slavery was morally wrong and should not be allowed to expand. He thought that blacks should be given the same basic opportunities as whites. Using a series of sophisticated legal arguments, he challenged Douglas's logic in the Kansas-Nebraska Act and especially Douglas's defense of the Dred Scott decision.

Lincoln, beardless before his presidency, often poked fun at his own appearance.

Lincoln also used his gift of humor to turn away other attacks. Once, Douglas called him a "two-faced man," suggesting that he said different things about slavery at different times. "I leave it to my audience," Lincoln responded. "If I had another face to wear, do you think I would wear this one?"

It rained on election day, but the turnout was good. In those days, people voted not for the candidates themselves, but for legislators committed to either of the two candidates. More people voted for Lincoln's delegates than for Douglas's. But because of the way the legislative districts were drawn, Douglas won. Comparing himself to a little boy who had stubbed his toe, Lincoln said, "It hurt too bad to laugh, and he was too big to cry."

Marines storming the engine-house at Harpers Ferry where John Brown was trapped

Despite the fact that he had lost the election, many newspapers in Illinois began regarding Lincoln as a candidate for president. As a leading spokesman of the Republican party, Lincoln continued making speeches against slavery but urging moderation on both sides. But moderate views were becoming harder to find.

On the night of October 16, 1859, a group of nineteen abolitionists led by John Brown attacked and seized a government armory in Harpers Ferry, Virginia (now West Virginia). During the uprising, the mayor of the Virginia town was killed. The action was part of Brown's plan to free slaves in Virginia by force and possibly set up a nation of freed slaves. The rebellion was quickly put down by a company of U.S. Marines led by Colonel Robert E. Lee, and ten of Brown's men were killed. Brown himself was hanged less than two months later.

Abraham Lincoln in 1858

In his speeches, Lincoln said that Brown was insane, but that he had also shown great courage. He urged calm. But he also warned the southern states, many now threatening to leave the Union. "If constitutionally we elect a President," Lincoln said, "and . . . you undertake to destroy the Union, it will be our duty to deal with you as old John Brown has been dealt with."

During the presidential campaign season of 1860, the Democratic party was torn apart. At two different meetings, southern Democrats walked out, eventually nominating their own candidate, John C. Breckinridge. The remaining Democrats chose the more moderate Stephen A. Douglas. Yet another group, the Constitutional Union party, nominated John Bell, a Whig from Tennessee.

The May 1860 Republican convention in Chicago, where Lincoln was nominated for president

In Chicago, more than ten thousand people crowded into a building nicknamed the Wigwam for the Republican convention held in May. Many of the delegates were for Lincoln, whom they nicknamed "the Rail-Splitter," recalling his days making rail fences in the wilderness. Other delegates, however, were for William H. Seward, a senator from New York. At home in Springfield, Lincoln heard about events at the convention by telegraph.

"We are dealing tenderly with delegates," one ally at the convention said in a telegram. Lincoln sent back his reply: "I authorize no bargains and will be bound by none." On the third ballot, Lincoln won the nomination. Hannibal Hamlin, a Maine senator, was named his vice-presidential running mate.

The Lincolns' home in Springfield on the morning of November 7, 1860

Lincoln made no speeches and never left Illinois during the campaign season. He did prepare a brief story about his life, which was published by two newspapers and sold more than a million copies. Although highly respected by many people in the North, Lincoln was hated and feared by many southerners. To his credit, Stephen A. Douglas made a number of speeches in the South, where he urged people not to leave the Union if Lincoln won the election.

On the night of November 6, 1860, Lincoln sat in the Springfield telegraph office and watched the reports of the election. With the Democratic party split, Lincoln won. He carried all eighteen free states but won not a single electoral vote in a slave state. It was an ominous sign.

"Well, boys," he said to the reporters gathered around him, "your troubles are over now; mine have just begun."

Opposite page: One of many Lincoln photographs taken by Mathew Brady

Chapter 5

The Sixteenth President

Early in the morning of February 11, 1861, a special train waited on the tracks at the Great Western railroad station in Springfield, Illinois. Although a bone-chilling rain was falling, more than a thousand people gathered in and around the station. They had come to say farewell to President-Elect Abraham Lincoln, who on the day before his fifty-second birthday, was about to begin a twelve-day journey to Washington, D.C.

Lincoln, who had started to grow a beard soon after his election, arrived at the train station with his oldest son, Robert. Mary and the couple's two younger sons stayed behind to take a later train to Indianapolis, where the family would be reunited to continue the journey east. At the Great Western station, Lincoln shook hands and talked quietly with his many well-wishers. Then he stepped onto the train and stood on the rear platform to bid farewell to his friends and neighbors of twenty-five years.

Opposite page: Lincoln, as president, with a beard. His eyes were gray.

Lincoln's Springfield house, where he lived until he became president

"My friends: No one, not in my situation, can appreciate my feeling of sadness at this parting," he said. "To this place, and the kindness of these people, I owe every thing. Here I have lived a quarter of a century, and have passed from a young to an old man. Here my children have been born, and one is buried. I now leave, not knowing when, or whether ever, I may return, with a task before me greater than that which rested upon Washington." After expressing his hope for guidance from the Divine Being, he added the words, "let us confidently hope that all will yet be well." He concluded the brief speech by saying, "I bid you an affectionate farewell."

Lincoln hoped that everything would yet work out for his troubled nation. But the situation grew worse each passing day. Just one week earlier, on February 4, delegates from seven of America's fifteen slaveholding states met in Montgomery, Alabama, to proclaim a new nation: the Confederate States of America. Other slaveholding states were threatening to secede from the Union as well.

As his train moved slowly eastward, Lincoln felt that he was now faced with the very task he believed impossible. He had to preserve a nation that was half slave and half free. He would gradually grow to feel that it could only be preserved if it were entirely free. But for the time being, he decided to draw a firm line on one issue. Despite the Supreme Court's Dred Scott ruling, he was determined to keep slavery from spreading into new territories or states. This stand infuriated slaveholders.

"Whether . . . Pennsylvania Avenue is paved ten fathoms deep with mangled bodies," howled Atlanta's Confederacy newspaper, "the South will never submit to the inauguration of Abraham Lincoln." The statement echoed the feelings of many southerners, and even some northerners. Soon it was found that there was at least one plot to assassinate Lincoln before his inauguration.

Allan Pinkerton, a detective assigned to protect the president-elect, discovered that a group of conspirators were planning to kill Lincoln at the Calvert Street train station in Baltimore. Reluctantly, he agreed to change trains secretly. Disguised as an invalid, the president-elect slipped unnoticed into Washington nine days before his inauguration. His family arrived separately.

A retouched pre-inaugural photograph taken by Mathew Brady on February 26, 1861

Heavily armed soldiers lined Pennsylvania Avenue in Washington on March 4, 1861, the day President Lincoln was inaugurated. Outgoing President Buchanan rode in a horse-drawn carriage to Lincoln's hotel. He greeted the new president by saying, "If you are as happy, my dear sir, on entering this house as I am on leaving it and returning home, you are the happiest man on earth."

The two men rode to the Capitol, where Lincoln spoke to the more than twenty thousand people who had gathered to watch and listen to the ceremony. In his inaugural address, Lincoln tried desperately to reassure southern slaveholders and avoid war. "I have no purpose, directly or indirectly, to interfere with the institution of

Chief Justice Taney administers the oath of office to Lincoln, March 4, 1861.

slavery in the States where it exists," he said. Promising to defend the Constitution, he tried to ease the enormous tensions of the time, saying, "There needs to be no bloodshed or violence; and there shall be none, unless it is forced upon the national authority."

In less than two weeks, while he patiently listened to the pleas of hordes of office-seekers, the dire threat of civil war was forced upon the president. By the time he was inaugurated on March 4, rebel forces had already captured many federal forts and armories throughout the Confederate states. On March 15, Lincoln learned that Fort Sumter in the harbor of Charleston, South Carolina, threatened by Confederate troops, was running out of supplies.

Hoping to avoid open warfare, the president sent a message to the governor of South Carolina a few weeks later. He informed the governor that a fleet of ships was being sent to bring food, not ammunition or fresh troops, to the fort. Despite Lincoln's attempt to ease tensions, early in the morning of April 12, 1861, Confederate soldiers fired on the fort. The Civil War had begun.

Lincoln immediately called for seventy-five thousand men to join the tiny Union Army for three months. He also called for an emergency session of Congress on July 4. Well before that date arrived, however, four more states joined the seven that had already seceded from the Union. Faced with a growing enemy made up of his own countrymen, Lincoln issued more emergency orders. He called for a naval blockade of the southern coast and suspended the right of *habeas corpus*, the constitutionally guaranteed right of Americans to protection from improper arrest. Union military commanders fighting in rebel states were given the right to try civilians in military courts. Lincoln also asked for more than forty-two thousand volunteers to join the Union Army for three years.

Many people offered to fight for the Union, but military officials were not prepared for the hordes of new recruits. Lincoln wrote that volunteers "rushed to the rescue of the government faster than the government [could] find arms to put in their hands." There were not enough guns, uniforms, or shoes for the rapidly growing army. There was also a shortage of trained officers. One of America's most able commanders had been Robert E. Lee, who left the Union to fight for the Confederacy. Many other fine

The Civil War battle of Bull Run on July 21, 1861

officers were fighting for the Confederacy as well. At the head of the Union forces was General Winfield Scott, once a competent leader but now seventy-five years old and nicknamed "Old Fuss 'n' Feathers."

Lincoln addressed a special session of Congress on July 4, 1861, pledging to hold the nation together by force. But two weeks later, a Union army was soundly defeated by Confederate troops near a little Virginia stream called Bull Run. The battle took place just thirty miles southwest of Washington, D.C. A few months later, Winfield Scott resigned and Lincoln gave his command to George B. McClellan, a railroad official in private life. Problems for the Union Army continued.

Major General George B. McClellan

Though McClellan organized the army well, he proved to be a cautious commander, continually calling for more reinforcements instead of fighting. Lincoln eventually fired him. To compound problems, the U.S. War Department was hampered by a number of corrupt and incompetent employees. When the department issued contracts to supply the army with provisions, shady deals were often made. Soldiers getting ready to fight for their country and their lives found themselves carrying rotten blankets and knapsacks that fell to pieces in the rain. In January 1862, Lincoln himself took control of the War Department, appointing a new leader and urging everyone to work harder. A few months later, he reorganized the Union Army as well.

The Battle of Shiloh, April 6 and 7, 1862, one of the bloodiest battles of the war

Confronted by the public tragedy of a nation at war with itself, Lincoln faced a private tragedy as well. In February 1862, his sons Willie and Tad developed serious fevers. Tad recovered, but Willie died on February 20. Lincoln suffered quietly, but Mary collapsed from sorrow and became mentally ill. From the grief-stricken White House, the president urged the Union Army to press the war effort. "This army has got to fight," he demanded. But when it did fight, the results were disastrous.

In April 1862, Union forces under the command of Ulysses S. Grant suffered thirteen thousand casualties during the Battle of Shiloh near Savannah, Tennessee. In August, the main Union Army was forced to retreat all the way to Washington when it lost a second battle at Bull Run. Attorney General Edward Bates recalled that Lincoln felt "almost ready to hang himself."

Lincoln meets with General McClellan and his company at Antietam, Maryland.

Since the first Battle of Bull Run, Union soldiers saw that the Confederates used slaves to carry weapons and otherwise help them in the war effort. Against strong objections from some representatives, Congress passed a confiscation bill permitting Union soldiers to seize slaves used by Confederate forces. These slaves were generally freed, many joining the Union Army.

On March 6, 1862, Lincoln made his first formal proposal to Congress designed to end slavery in America. The plan involved the gradual freeing of slaves, payments to white owners for their losses, and the establishment of new colonies outside the United States for liberated slaves. Although some congressmen objected to the plan and it never passed, other measures were put forth that weakened the legal position of slaveholders.

A week after he made his first emancipation proposal, Lincoln signed into law a bill forbidding the return of runaway slaves to their former homes in Confederate states. In June 1862, Congress passed a bill overturning the Dred Scott decision by outlawing human bondage in all federal territories (but not in existing states).

The following month, July, Congress and the president worked out the details of a far-reaching confiscation bill that, eventually, would have freed many slaves. According to the new law, if the rebellion in the South did not end in sixty days, anyone who helped it could have their property, including their slaves, seized by the Union government. These acts of seizure were to be determined by the federal court system on a case-by-case basis.

All of these laws, created to move the country gradually toward emancipation, became unimportant when Lincoln issued the preliminary Emancipation Proclamation late in September 1862. Abolitionists as well as free and enslaved blacks cheered the news. But not everyone, even in the North, approved. Union Democrats stirred up racial fears among many northern whites, leading to a Republican disaster in the congressional elections of 1862. Now Republicans held only a narrow majority in Congress.

The war, of course, didn't stop for elections or presidential proclamations. Early in 1863, near the Virginia cities of Fredericksburg and Chancellorsville, the Union Army suffered two more defeats. In July, the bloodiest and most decisive battle of the war was fought near Gettysburg, Pennsylvania. The three-day battle left five thousand men dead, though the Confederates were forced to retreat.

GETTYSBURG ADDRESS

Four score and seven years ago our fathers brought forth on this continent, a new nation, conceived in Liberty, and dedicated to the proposition that all men are created equal.

Now we are engaged in a great civil war, testing whether that nation, or any nation so conceived and so dedicated, can long endure. We are met on a great battle-field of that war. We have come to dedicate a portion of that field, as a final resting place for those who here gave their lives that that nation might live. It is altogether fitting and proper that we should do this.

But, in a larger sense, we can not dedicate—we can not consecrate—we can not hallow—this ground. The brave men, living and dead, who struggled here, have consecrated it, far above our poor power to add or detract. The world will little note, nor long remember what we say here, but it can never forget what they did here. It is for us the living, rather, to be dedicated here to the unfinished work which they who fought here have thus far so nobly advanced. It is rather for us to be here dedicated to the great task remaining before us—that from these honored dead we take increased devotion to that cause for which they gave the last full measure of devotion—that we here highly resolve that these dead shall not have died in vain—that this nation, under God, shall have a new birth of freedom—and that government of the people, by the people, for the people, shall not perish from the earth.

On November 19, 1863, Lincoln traveled to the battleground to dedicate a national cemetery. There, barely noticed by some after a two-hour speech by a well-known orator, Lincoln delivered his Gettysburg Address, just ten sentences in length. In those few words, he reminded the nation and the world why the war was being fought.

Less than a week after Lincoln gave his speech, a Union army under Ulysses S. Grant defeated Confederate troops near Chattanooga, Tennessee, and eventually forced all rebel forces from that state. Soon Grant was put in charge of all Union troops. But as he was attempting to advance toward Richmond, Virginia, Grant's army met fierce resistance and was stalemated for nearly a year.

Edward Everett (right), one of
the greatest orators of the day,
spoke for two hours at the
ceremony to dedicate the
national cemetery at Gettysburg.
Afterwards, Lincoln (below) delivered
his famous Gettysburg Address,
speaking for only about three minutes.

A Confederate sharpshooter killed at Gettysburg

While Grant and his soldiers remained in Virginia, America approached another presidential election, scheduled for November 8, 1864. On June 8, the Republican party nominated Lincoln for a second term. Andrew Johnson, who was serving as the military governor of Tennessee, was chosen as his running mate. George B. McClellan, whom Lincoln had fired as the leader of the Union Army, was nominated by the Democrats.

Although the president felt certain that he could not win a second term, Union armies won substantial victories in the months leading up to the election. Union general William Sherman captured Atlanta and was preparing to march through the South to the sea. To a war-weary nation, it seemed the fighting would soon be over. Lincoln was reelected in November by a comfortable margin.

When the elections were over, Lincoln and Congress turned their attention to some historic unfinished business. The Emancipation Proclamation freed only those slaves who lived in Confederate territory. Slaves in states that had remained loyal to the Union were still legally in bondage. Lincoln and a number of congressional leaders now wanted to propose a new amendment to the Constitution that would outlaw slavery everywhere in America. But an earlier effort had already failed to pass the House of Representatives.

Lincoln had once said, "If slavery is not wrong, nothing is wrong." The president's words were repeated in Congress, where the Senate approved the amendment, but the House still seemed unable to gather enough votes for passage. Finally, Lincoln and a few other pro-amendment politicians held secret meetings with representatives unwilling to vote for the amendment. To this day, the offers Lincoln made have never been made public. But according to Lincoln biographer Stephen B. Oates, they "allegedly involved patronage, a New Jersey railroad monopoly, and the release of rebels kin to congressional Democrats."

The amendment eventually passed and was adopted in December 1865. According to Representative Thaddeus Stevens, "The greatest measure of the nineteenth century was passed by corruption, aided and abetted by the purest man in America." To become the Thirteenth Amendment, the measure had to be ratified by the states, which it eventually was. In this strange way, slavery in America was finally outlawed.

**Above: Confederate general Robert E. Lee (front, white hair) and his generals
Below: Union general Ulysses S. Grant (center left, against tree) and his staff**

This regiment of the Army of the Potomac included a former slave.

By March 4, 1865, when Lincoln took his second oath of office, the Civil War was nearly over. In his second inaugural address, Lincoln made it clear that he wanted to quickly forgive the states that were still in rebellion.

"Fondly do we hope—fervently do we pray—that this mighty scourge of war may speedily pass away," he said. "With malice toward none, with charity for all; . . . let us strive on to finish the work we are in; to bind up the nation's wounds; . . . to do all which may achieve and cherish a just, and a lasting, peace. . . ."

Just thirty-six days later, on April 9, 1865, the South's Robert E. Lee surrendered to the North's Ulysses S. Grant to end the American Civil War. As much as ever before, the United States needed Lincoln's leadership. More than anyone else, Lincoln planned to welcome the rebel states back into the Union with kindness and understanding. But history took one more cruel turn.

Chapter 6

Good Friday

"I shall never live to see peace," Lincoln once told the writer Harriet Beecher Stowe. "This war is killing me."

By the early months of 1865, anyone who had known the president for long had to agree. Always tall and thin, Lincoln had lost at least twenty-five pounds during the Civil War. His face, creased with lines of worry, looked decades older than it had just a few years earlier.

Nearly 620,000 Americans died in the endless battles of the Civil War, and the strain appeared to be more than the president could stand. Still, wounded as it was, the nation was whole again.

Five days after the Civil War ended, Christians around the nation celebrated Good Friday, the anniversary of the crucifixion of Jesus. That morning, April 14, 1865, President Lincoln, his cabinet, and General Grant discussed how the military occupation of the South could be handled without cruelty. That evening, with Mrs. Lincoln, he traveled a few blocks east of the White House to Ford's Theater. There they entered a private box to watch a humorous play called *Our American Cousin*.

Opposite page: Photograph of Lincoln taken
on April 9, 1865, the Sunday before his death

85

As the third act of the play was in progress, at about 10:00, John Wilkes Booth, a member of a well-known family of actors, entered the private box. Booth carried a dagger in one hand and a small, single-shot derringer in the other. He put the pistol to President Lincoln's head and fired. As Lincoln slumped unconscious in his rocking chair, Booth jumped from the box onto the stage.

"*Sic semper tyrannis*," Booth shouted, Latin for "Thus always to tyrants." Then Booth fled the stage and escaped on a horse waiting outside the theater. He was shot and killed several days later by a cavalry trooper while trapped in a burning barn. Booth had been part of a conspiracy to kill the president and other government officials.

Inside the theater, Doctor Charles Leale rushed from his seat on the main floor, examined the president's head wound, and said, "It is impossible for him to recover." Lincoln was carried out of the theater to a nearby house, where he was placed in a bed on the first floor. For about nine hours, his unconscious body was surrounded by cabinet members, physicians, and surgeons. Mrs. Lincoln and the Lincolns' son Robert were also nearby. At 7:22 on the morning of April 15, 1865, the president died.

Controversial during his presidency, Lincoln was mourned by a nation beginning to realize clearly what he had done for his country. More than six million people turned out to view the special train that carried his body back to Springfield, Illinois, to be buried. "A greater work is seldom performed by a single man," the Reverend James Reed said of the fallen leader. "Generations yet unborn will rise up and call him blessed."

Above: President Lincoln is assassinated at Ford's Theater.
Below: Government officials surround Lincoln on his deathbed.

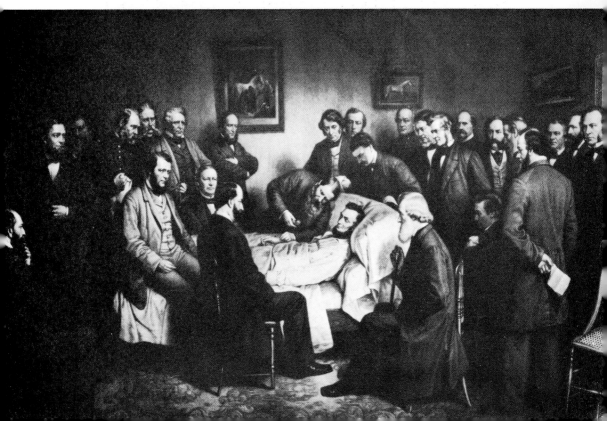

Above: Lincoln with his son Tad in 1864, the only known photograph of Lincoln wearing glasses. **Opposite page:** Photograph of Lincoln taken on April 10, 1865, the Monday before he died. The negative photographic plate was broken; hence the line across the top.

Chronology of American History

(Shaded area covers events in Abraham Lincoln's lifetime.)

About A.D. 982—Eric the Red, born in Norway, reaches Greenland in one of the first European voyages to North America.

About 1000—Leif Ericson (Eric the Red's son) leads what is thought to be the first European expedition to mainland North America; Leif probably lands in Canada.

1492—Christopher Columbus, seeking a sea route from Spain to the Far East, discovers the New World.

1497—John Cabot reaches Canada in the first English voyage to North America.

1513—Ponce de Léon explores Florida in search of the fabled Fountain of Youth.

1519-1521—Hernando Cortés of Spain conquers Mexico.

1534—French explorers led by Jacques Cartier enter the Gulf of St. Lawrence in Canada.

1540—Spanish explorer Francisco Coronado begins exploring the American Southwest, seeking the riches of the mythical Seven Cities of Cibola.

1565—St. Augustine, Florida, the first permanent European town in what is now the United States, is founded by the Spanish.

1607—Jamestown, Virginia, is founded, the first permanent English town in the present-day U.S.

1608—Frenchman Samuel de Champlain founds the village of Quebec, Canada.

1609—Henry Hudson explores the eastern coast of present-day U.S. for the Netherlands; the Dutch then claim parts of New York, New Jersey, Delaware, and Connecticut and name the area New Netherland.

1619—The English colonies' first shipment of black slaves arrives in Jamestown.

1620—English Pilgrims found Massachusetts' first permanent town at Plymouth.

1621—Massachusetts Pilgrims and Indians hold the famous first Thanksgiving feast in colonial America.

1623—Colonization of New Hampshire is begun by the English.

1624—Colonization of present-day New York State is begun by the Dutch at Fort Orange (Albany).

1625—The Dutch start building New Amsterdam (now New York City).

1630—The town of Boston, Massachusetts, is founded by the English Puritans.

1633—Colonization of Connecticut is begun by the English.

1634—Colonization of Maryland is begun by the English.

1636—Harvard, the colonies' first college, is founded in Massachusetts. Rhode Island colonization begins when Englishman Roger Williams founds Providence.

1638—Delaware colonization begins as Swedes build Fort Christina at present-day Wilmington.

1640—Stephen Daye of Cambridge, Massachusetts prints *The Bay Psalm Book*, the first English-language book published in what is now the U.S.

1643—Swedish settlers begin colonizing Pennsylvania.

About 1650—North Carolina is colonized by Virginia settlers.

1660—New Jersey colonization is begun by the Dutch at present-day Jersey City.

1670—South Carolina colonization is begun by the English near Charleston.

1673—Jacques Marquette and Louis Jolliet explore the upper Mississippi River for France.

1682—Philadelphia, Pennsylvania, is settled. La Salle explores Mississippi River all the way to its mouth in Louisiana and claims the whole Mississippi Valley for France.

1693—College of William and Mary is founded in Williamsburg, Virginia.

1700—Colonial population is about 250,000.

1703—Benjamin Franklin is born in Boston.

1732—George Washington, first president of the U.S., is born in Westmoreland County, Virginia.

1733—James Oglethorpe founds Savannah, Georgia; Georgia is established as the thirteenth colony.

1735—John Adams, second president of the U.S., is born in Braintree, Massachusetts.

1737—William Byrd founds Richmond, Virginia.

1738—British troops are sent to Georgia over border dispute with Spain.

1739—Black insurrection takes place in South Carolina.

1740—English Parliament passes act allowing naturalization of immigrants to American colonies after seven-year residence.

1743—Thomas Jefferson is born in Albemarle County, Virginia. Benjamin Franklin retires at age thirty-seven to devote himself to scientific inquiries and public service.

1744—King George's War begins; France joins war effort against England.

1745—During King George's War, France raids settlements in Maine and New York.

1747—Classes begin at Princeton College in New Jersey.

1748—The Treaty of Aix-la-Chapelle concludes King George's War.

1749—Parliament legally recognizes slavery in colonies and the inauguration of the plantation system in the South. George Washington becomes the surveyor for Culpepper County in Virginia.

1750—Thomas Walker passes through and names Cumberland Gap on his way toward Kentucky region. Colonial population is about 1,200,000.

1751—James Madison, fourth president of the U.S., is born in Port Conway, Virginia. English Parliament passes Currency Act, banning New England colonies from issuing paper money. George Washington travels to Barbados.

1752—Pennsylvania Hospital, the first general hospital in the colonies, is founded in Philadelphia. Benjamin Franklin uses a kite in a thunderstorm to demonstrate that lightning is a form of electricity.

1753—George Washington delivers command that the French withdraw from the Ohio River Valley; French disregard the demand. Colonial population is about 1,328,000.

1754—French and Indian War begins (extends to Europe as the Seven Years' War). Washington surrenders at Fort Necessity.

1755—French and Indians ambush Braddock. Washington becomes commander of Virginia troops.

1756—England declares war on France.

1758—James Monroe, fifth president of the U.S., is born in Westmoreland County, Virginia.

1759—Cherokee Indian war begins in southern colonies; hostilities extend to 1761. George Washington marries Martha Dandridge Custis.

1760—George III becomes king of England. Colonial population is about 1,600,000.

1762—England declares war on Spain.

1763—Treaty of Paris concludes the French and Indian War and the Seven Years' War. England gains Canada and most other French lands east of the Mississippi River.

1764—British pass the Sugar Act to gain tax money from the colonists. The issue of taxation without representation is first introduced in Boston. John Adams marries Abigail Smith.

1765—Stamp Act goes into effect in the colonies. Business virtually stops as almost all colonists refuse to use the stamps.

1766—British repeal the Stamp Act.

1767 — John Quincy Adams, sixth president of the U.S. and son of second president John Adams, is born in Braintree, Massachusetts. Andrew Jackson, seventh president of the U.S., is born in Waxhaw settlement, South Carolina.

1769 — Daniel Boone sights the Kentucky Territory.

1770 — In the Boston Massacre, British soldiers kill five colonists and injure six. Townshend Acts are repealed, thus eliminating all duties on imports to the colonies except tea.

1771 — Benjamin Franklin begins his autobiography, a work that he will never complete. The North Carolina assembly passes the "Bloody Act," which makes rioters guilty of treason.

1772 — Samuel Adams rouses colonists to consider British threats to self-government.

1773 — English Parliament passes the Tea Act. Colonists dressed as Mohawk Indians board British tea ships and toss 342 casks of tea into the water in what becomes known as the Boston Tea Party. William Henry Harrison is born in Charles City County, Virginia.

1774 — British close the port of Boston to punish the city for the Boston Tea Party. First Continental Congress convenes in Philadelphia.

1775 — American Revolution begins with battles of Lexington and Concord, Massachusetts. Second Continental Congress opens in Philadelphia. George Washington becomes commander-in-chief of the Continental army.

1776 — Declaration of Independence is adopted on July 4.

1777 — Congress adopts the American flag with thirteen stars and thirteen stripes. John Adams is sent to France to negotiate peace treaty.

1778 — France declares war against Great Britain and becomes U.S. ally.

1779 — British surrender to Americans at Vincennes. Thomas Jefferson is elected governor of Virginia. James Madison is elected to the Continental Congress.

1780 — Benedict Arnold, first American traitor, defects to the British.

1781 — Articles of Confederation go into effect. Cornwallis surrenders to George Washington at Yorktown, ending the American Revolution.

1782 — American commissioners, including John Adams, sign peace treaty with British in Paris. Thomas Jefferson's wife, Martha, dies. Martin Van Buren is born in Kinderhook, New York.

1784 — Zachary Taylor is born near Barboursville, Virginia.

1785 — Congress adopts the dollar as the unit of currency. John Adams is made minister to Great Britain. Thomas Jefferson is appointed minister to France.

1786 — Shays's Rebellion begins in Massachusetts.

1787 — Constitutional Convention assembles in Philadelphia, with George Washington presiding; U.S. Constitution is adopted. Delaware, New Jersey, and Pennsylvania become states.

1788 — Virginia, South Carolina, New York, Connecticut, New Hampshire, Maryland, and Massachusetts become states. U.S. Constitution is ratified. New York City is declared U.S. capital.

1789 — Presidential electors elect George Washington and John Adams as first president and vice-president. Thomas Jefferson is appointed secretary of state. North Carolina becomes a state. French Revolution begins.

1790 — Supreme Court meets for the first time. Rhode Island becomes a state. First national census in the U.S. counts 3,929,214 persons. John Tyler is born in Charles City County, Virginia.

1791 — Vermont enters the Union. U.S. Bill of Rights, the first ten amendments to the Constitution, goes into effect. District of Columbia is established. James Buchanan is born in Stony Batter, Pennsylvania.

1792 — Thomas Paine publishes *The Rights of Man*. Kentucky becomes a state. Two political parties are formed in the U.S., Federalist and Republican. Washington is elected to a second term, with Adams as vice-president.

1793 — War between France and Britain begins; U.S. declares neutrality. Eli Whitney invents the cotton gin; cotton production and slave labor increase in the South.

1794—Eleventh Amendment to the Constitution is passed, limiting federal courts' power. "Whiskey Rebellion" in Pennsylvania protests federal whiskey tax. James Madison marries Dolley Payne Todd.

1795—George Washington signs the Jay Treaty with Great Britain. Treaty of San Lorenzo, between U.S. and Spain, settles Florida boundary and gives U.S. right to navigate the Mississippi. James Polk is born near Pineville, North Carolina.

1796—Tennessee enters the Union. Washington gives his Farewell Address, refusing a third presidential term. John Adams is elected president and Thomas Jefferson vice-president.

1797—Adams recommends defense measures against possible war with France. Napoleon Bonaparte and his army march against Austrians in Italy. U.S. population is about 4,900,000.

1798—Washington is named commander-in-chief of the U.S. Army. Department of the Navy is created. Alien and Sedition Acts are passed. Napoleon's troops invade Egypt and Switzerland.

1799—George Washington dies at Mount Vernon, New York. James Monroe is elected governor of Virginia. French Revolution ends. Napoleon becomes ruler of France.

1800—Thomas Jefferson and Aaron Burr tie for president. U.S. capital is moved from Philadelphia to Washington, D.C. The White House is built as presidents' home. Spain returns Louisiana to France. Millard Fillmore is born in Locke, New York.

1801—After thirty-six ballots, House of Representatives elects Thomas Jefferson president, making Burr vice-president. James Madison is named secretary of state.

1802—Congress abolishes excise taxes. U.S. Military Academy is founded at West Point, New York.

1803—Ohio enters the Union. Louisiana Purchase treaty is signed with France, greatly expanding U.S. territory.

1804—Twelfth Amendment to the Constitution rules that president and vice-president be elected separately. Alexander Hamilton is killed by Vice-President Aaron Burr in a duel. Orleans Territory is established. Napoleon crowns himself emperor of France. Franklin Pierce is born in Hillsborough Lower Village, New Hampshire.

1805—Thomas Jefferson begins his second term as president. Lewis and Clark expedition reaches the Pacific Ocean.

1806—Coinage of silver dollars is stopped; resumes in 1836.

1807—Aaron Burr is acquitted in treason trial. Embargo Act closes U.S. ports to trade.

1808—James Madison is elected president. Congress outlaws importing slaves from Africa. Andrew Johnson is born in Raleigh, North Carolina.

1809—Abraham Lincoln is born near Hodgenville, Kentucky.

1810—U.S. population is 7,240,000.

1811—William Henry Harrison defeats Indians at Tippecanoe. Monroe is named secretary of state.

1812—Louisiana becomes a state. U.S. declares war on Britain (War of 1812). James Madison is reelected president. Napoleon invades Russia.

1813—British forces take Fort Niagara and Buffalo, New York.

1814—Francis Scott Key writes "The Star-Spangled Banner." British troops burn much of Washington, D.C., including the White House. Treaty of Ghent ends War of 1812. James Monroe becomes secretary of war.

1815—Napoleon meets his final defeat at Battle of Waterloo.

1816—James Monroe is elected president. Indiana becomes a state.

1817—Mississippi becomes a state. Construction on Erie Canal begins.

1818—Illinois enters the Union. The present thirteen-stripe flag is adopted. Border between U.S. and Canada is agreed upon.

1819—Alabama becomes a state. U.S. purchases Florida from Spain. Thomas Jefferson establishes the University of Virginia.

1820—James Monroe is reelected. In the Missouri Compromise, Maine enters the Union as a free (non-slave) state.

1821—Missouri enters the Union as a slave state. Santa Fe Trail opens the American Southwest. Mexico declares independence from Spain. Napoleon Bonaparte dies.

1822—U.S. recognizes Mexico and Colombia. Liberia in Africa is founded as a home for freed slaves. Ulysses S. Grant is born in Point Pleasant, Ohio. Rutherford B. Hayes is born in Delaware, Ohio.

1823—Monroe Doctrine closes North and South America to European colonizing or invasion.

1824—House of Representatives elects John Quincy Adams president when none of the four candidates wins a majority in national election. Mexico becomes a republic.

1825—Erie Canal is opened. U.S. population is 11,300,000.

1826—Thomas Jefferson and John Adams both die on July 4, the fiftieth anniversary of the Declaration of Independence.

1828—Andrew Jackson is elected president. Tariff of Abominations is passed, cutting imports.

1829—James Madison attends Virginia's constitutional convention. Slavery is abolished in Mexico. Chester A. Arthur is born in Fairfield, Vermont.

1830—Indian Removal Act to resettle Indians west of the Mississippi is approved.

1831—James Monroe dies in New York City. James A. Garfield is born in Orange, Ohio. Cyrus McCormick develops his reaper.

1832—Andrew Jackson, nominated by the new Democratic Party, is reelected president.

1833—Britain abolishes slavery in its colonies. Benjamin Harrison is born in North Bend, Ohio.

1835—Federal government becomes debt-free for the first time.

1836—Martin Van Buren becomes president. Texas wins independence from Mexico. Arkansas joins the Union. James Madison dies at Montpelier, Virginia.

1837—Michigan enters the Union. U.S. population is 15,900,000. Grover Cleveland is born in Caldwell, New Jersey.

1840—William Henry Harrison is elected president.

1841—President Harrison dies in Washington, D.C., one month after inauguration. Vice-President John Tyler succeeds him.

1843—William McKinley is born in Niles, Ohio.

1844—James Knox Polk is elected president. Samuel Morse sends first telegraphic message.

1845—Texas and Florida become states. Potato famine in Ireland causes massive emigration from Ireland to U.S. Andrew Jackson dies near Nashville, Tennessee.

1846—Iowa enters the Union. War with Mexico begins.

1847—U.S. captures Mexico City.

1848—Zachary Taylor becomes president. Treaty of Guadalupe Hidalgo ends Mexico-U.S. war. Wisconsin becomes a state.

1849—James Polk dies in Nashville, Tennessee.

1850—President Taylor dies in Washington, D.C.; Vice-President Millard Fillmore succeeds him. California enters the Union, breaking tie between slave and free states.

1852—Franklin Pierce is elected president.

1853—Gadsden Purchase transfers Mexican territory to U.S.

1854—"War for Bleeding Kansas" is fought between slave and free states.

1855—Czar Nicholas I of Russia dies, succeeded by Alexander II.

1856—James Buchanan is elected president. In Massacre of Potawatomi Creek, Kansas-slavers are murdered by free-staters. Woodrow Wilson is born in Staunton, Pennsylvania.

1857—William Howard Taft is born in Cincinnati, Ohio.

1858—Minnesota enters the Union. Theodore Roosevelt is born in New York City.

1859—Oregon becomes a state.

1860—Abraham Lincoln is elected president; South Carolina secedes from the Union in protest.

1861—Arkansas, Tennessee, North Carolina, and Virginia secede. Kansas enters the Union as a free state. Civil War begins.

1862—Union forces capture Fort Henry, Roanoke Island, Fort Donelson, Jacksonville, and New Orleans; Union armies are defeated at the battles of Bull Run and Fredericksburg. Martin Van Buren dies in Kinderhook, New York. John Tyler dies near Charles City, Virginia.

1863—Lincoln issues Emancipation Proclamation: all slaves held in rebelling territories are declared free. West Virginia becomes a state.

1864—Abraham Lincoln is reelected. Nevada becomes a state.

1865—Lincoln is assassinated in Washington, D.C., and succeeded by Andrew Johnson. U.S. Civil War ends on May 26. Thirteenth Amendment abolishes slavery. Warren G. Harding is born in Blooming Grove, Ohio.

1867—Nebraska becomes a state. U.S. buys Alaska from Russia for $7,200,000. Reconstruction Acts are passed.

1868—President Johnson is impeached for violating Tenure of Office Act, but is acquitted by Senate. Ulysses S. Grant is elected president. Fourteenth Amendment prohibits voting discrimination. James Buchanan dies in Lancaster, Pennsylvania.

1869—Franklin Pierce dies in Concord, New Hampshire.

1870—Fifteenth Amendment gives blacks the right to vote.

1872—Grant is reelected over Horace Greeley. General Amnesty Act pardons ex-Confederates. Calvin Coolidge is born in Plymouth Notch, Vermont.

1874—Millard Fillmore dies in Buffalo, New York. Herbert Hoover is born in West Branch, Iowa.

1875—Andrew Johnson dies in Carter's Station, Tennessee.

1876—Colorado enters the Union. "Custer's last stand": he and his men are massacred by Sioux Indians at Little Big Horn, Montana.

1877—Rutherford B. Hayes is elected president as all disputed votes are awarded to him.

1880—James A. Garfield is elected president.

1881—President Garfield is assassinated and dies in Elberon, New Jersey. Vice-President Chester A. Arthur succeeds him.

1882—U.S. bans Chinese immigration. Franklin D. Roosevelt is born in Hyde Park, New York.

1884—Grover Cleveland is elected president.

1885—Ulysses S. Grant dies in Mount McGregor, New York.

1886—Statue of Liberty is dedicated. Chester A. Arthur dies in New York City.

1888—Benjamin Harrison is elected president.

1889—North Dakota, South Dakota, Washington, and Montana become states.

1890—Dwight D. Eisenhower is born in Denison, Texas. Idaho and Wyoming become states.

1892—Grover Cleveland is elected president.

1893—Rutherford B. Hayes dies in Fremont, Ohio.

1896—William McKinley is elected president. Utah becomes a state.

1898—U.S. declares war on Spain over Cuba.

1900—McKinley is reelected. Boxer Rebellion against foreigners in China begins.

1901—McKinley is assassinated by anarchist Leon Czolgosz in Buffalo, New York; Theodore Roosevelt becomes president. Benjamin Harrison dies in Indianapolis, Indiana.

1902—U.S. acquires perpetual control over Panama Canal.

1903—Alaskan frontier is settled.

1904—Russian-Japanese War breaks out. Theodore Roosevelt wins presidential election.

1905 — Treaty of Portsmouth signed, ending Russian-Japanese War.

1906 — U.S. troops occupy Cuba.

1907 — President Roosevelt bars all Japanese immigration. Oklahoma enters the Union.

1908 — William Howard Taft becomes president. Grover Cleveland dies in Princeton, New Jersey. Lyndon B. Johnson is born near Stonewall, Texas.

1909 — NAACP is founded under W.E.B. DuBois

1910 — China abolishes slavery.

1911 — Chinese Revolution begins. Ronald Reagan is born in Tampico, Illinois.

1912 — Woodrow Wilson is elected president. Arizona and New Mexico become states.

1913 — Federal income tax is introduced in U.S. through the Sixteenth Amendment. Richard Nixon is born in Yorba Linda, California. Gerald Ford is born in Omaha, Nebraska.

1914 — World War I begins.

1915 — British liner *Lusitania* is sunk by German submarine.

1916 — Wilson is reelected president.

1917 — U.S. breaks diplomatic relations with Germany. Czar Nicholas of Russia abdicates as revolution begins. U.S. declares war on Austria-Hungary. John F. Kennedy is born in Brookline, Massachusetts.

1918 — Wilson proclaims "Fourteen Points" as war aims. On November 11, armistice is signed between Allies and Germany.

1919 — Eighteenth Amendment prohibits sale and manufacture of intoxicating liquors. Wilson presides over first League of Nations; wins Nobel Peace Prize. Theodore Roosevelt dies in Oyster Bay, New York.

1920 — Nineteenth Amendment (women's suffrage) is passed. Warren Harding is elected president.

1921 — Adolf Hitler's stormtroopers begin to terrorize political opponents.

1922 — Irish Free State is established. Soviet states form USSR. Benito Mussolini forms Fascist government in Italy.

1923 — President Harding dies in San Francisco, California; he is succeeded by Vice-President Calvin Coolidge.

1924 — Coolidge is elected president. Woodrow Wilson dies in Washington, D.C. James Carter is born in Plains, Georgia.

1925 — Hitler reorganizes Nazi Party and publishes first volume of *Mein Kampf.*

1926 — Fascist youth organizations founded in Germany and Italy. Republic of Lebanon proclaimed.

1927 — Stalin becomes Soviet dictator. Economic conference in Geneva attended by fifty-two nations.

1928 — Herbert Hoover is elected president. U.S. and many other nations sign Kellogg-Briand pacts to outlaw war.

1929 — Stock prices in New York crash on "Black Thursday"; the Great Depression begins.

1930 — Bank of U.S. and its many branches close (most significant bank failure of the year). William Howard Taft dies in Washington, D.C.

1931 — Emigration from U.S. exceeds immigration for first time as Depression deepens.

1932 — Franklin D. Roosevelt wins presidential election in a Democratic landslide.

1933 — First concentration camps are erected in Germany. U.S. recognizes USSR and resumes trade. Twenty-First Amendment repeals prohibition. Calvin Coolidge dies in Northampton, Massachusetts.

1934 — Severe dust storms hit Plains states. President Roosevelt passes U.S. Social Security Act.

1936 — Roosevelt is reelected. Spanish Civil War begins. Hitler and Mussolini form Rome-Berlin Axis.

1937 — Roosevelt signs Neutrality Act.

1938 — Roosevelt sends appeal to Hitler and Mussolini to settle European problems amicably.

1939 — Germany takes over Czechoslovakia and invades Poland, starting World War II.

1940 — Roosevelt is reelected for a third term.

1941 — Japan bombs Pearl Harbor, U.S. declares war on Japan. Germany and Italy declare war on U.S.; U.S. then declares war on them.

1942 — Allies agree not to make separate peace treaties with the enemies. U.S. government transfers more than 100,000 Nisei (Japanese-Americans) from west coast to inland concentration camps.

1943 — Allied bombings of Germany begin.

1944 — Roosevelt is reelected for a fourth term. Allied forces invade Normandy on D-Day.

1945 — President Franklin D. Roosevelt dies in Warm Springs, Georgia; Vice-President Harry S. Truman succeeds him. Mussolini is killed; Hitler commits suicide. Germany surrenders. U.S. drops atomic bomb on Hiroshima; Japan surrenders: end of World War II.

1946 — U.N. General Assembly holds its first session in London. Peace conference of twenty-one nations is held in Paris.

1947 — Peace treaties are signed in Paris. "Cold War" is in full swing.

1948 — U.S. passes Marshall Plan Act, providing $17 billion in aid for Europe. U.S. recognizes new nation of Israel. India and Pakistan become free of British rule. Truman is elected president.

1949 — Republic of Eire is proclaimed in Dublin. Russia blocks land route access from Western Germany to Berlin; airlift begins. U.S., France, and Britain agree to merge their zones of occupation in West Germany. Apartheid program begins in South Africa.

1950 — Riots in Johannesburg, South Africa, against apartheid. North Korea invades South Korea. U.N. forces land in South Korea and recapture Seoul.

1951 — Twenty-Second Amendment limits president to two terms.

1952 — Dwight D. Eisenhower resigns as supreme commander in Europe and is elected president.

1953 — Stalin dies; struggle for power in Russia follows. Rosenbergs are executed for espionage.

1954 — U.S. and Japan sign mutual defense agreement.

1955 — Blacks in Montgomery, Alabama, boycott segregated bus lines.

1956 — Eisenhower is reelected president. Soviet troops march into Hungary.

1957 — U.S. agrees to withdraw ground forces from Japan. Russia launches first satellite, *Sputnik*.

1958 — European Common Market comes into being. Alaska becomes the forty-ninth state. Fidel Castro begins war against Batista government in Cuba.

1959 — Hawaii becomes fiftieth state. Castro becomes premier of Cuba. De Gaulle is proclaimed president of the Fifth Republic of France.

1960 — Historic debates between Senator John F. Kennedy and Vice-President Richard Nixon are televised. Kennedy is elected president. Brezhnev becomes president of USSR.

1961 — Berlin Wall is constructed. Kennedy and Khrushchev confer in Vienna. In Bay of Pigs incident, Cubans trained by CIA attempt to overthrow Castro.

1962 — U.S. military council is established in South Vietnam.

1963 — Riots and beatings by police and whites mark civil rights demonstrations in Birmingham, Alabama; 30,000 troops are called out, Martin Luther King, Jr., is arrested. Freedom marchers descend on Washington, D.C., to demonstrate. President Kennedy is assassinated in Dallas, Texas; Vice-President Lyndon B. Johnson is sworn in as president.

1964 — U.S. aircraft bomb North Vietnam. Johnson is elected president. Herbert Hoover dies in New York City.

1965 — U.S. combat troops arrive in South Vietnam.

1966 — Thousands protest U.S. policy in Vietnam. National Guard quells race riots in Chicago.

1967 — Six-Day War between Israel and Arab nations.

1968 — Martin Luther King, Jr., is assassinated in Memphis, Tennessee. Senator Robert Kennedy is assassinated in Los Angeles. Riots and police brutality take place at Democratic National Convention in Chicago. Richard Nixon is elected president. Czechoslovakia is invaded by Soviet troops.

1969—Dwight D. Eisenhower dies in Washington, D.C. Hundreds of thousands of people in several U.S. cities demonstrate against Vietnam War.

1970—Four Vietnam War protesters are killed by National Guardsmen at Kent State University in Ohio.

1971—Twenty-Sixth Amendment allows eighteen-year-olds to vote.

1972—Nixon visits Communist China; is reelected president in near-record landslide. Watergate affair begins when five men are arrested in the Watergate hotel complex in Washington, D.C. Nixon announces resignations of aides Haldeman, Ehrlichman, and Dean and Attorney General Kleindienst as a result of Watergate-related charges. Harry S. Truman dies in Kansas City, Missouri.

1973—Vice-President Spiro Agnew resigns; Gerald Ford is named vice-president. Vietnam peace treaty is formally approved after nineteen months of negotiations. Lyndon B. Johnson dies in San Antonio, Texas.

1974—As a result of Watergate cover-up, impeachment is considered; Nixon resigns and Ford becomes president. Ford pardons Nixon and grants limited amnesty to Vietnam War draft evaders and military deserters.

1975—U.S. civilians are evacuated from Saigon, South Vietnam, as Communist forces complete takeover of South Vietnam.

1976—U.S. celebrates its Bicentennial. James Earl Carter becomes president.

1977—Carter pardons most Vietnam draft evaders, numbering some 10,000.

1980—Ronald Reagan is elected president.

1981—President Reagan is shot in the chest in assassination attempt. Sandra Day O'Connor is appointed first woman justice of the Supreme Court.

1983—U.S. troops invade island of Grenada.

1984—Reagan is reelected president. Democratic candidate Walter Mondale's running mate, Geraldine Ferraro, is the first woman selected for vice-president by a major U.S. political party.

1985—Soviet Communist Party secretary Konstantin Chernenko dies; Mikhail Gorbachev succeeds him. U.S. and Soviet officials discuss arms control in Geneva. Reagan and Gorbachev hold summit conference in Geneva. Racial tensions accelerate in South Africa.

1986—Space shuttle *Challenger* explodes shortly after takeoff; crew of seven dies. U.S. bombs bases in Libya. Corazon Aquino defeats Ferdinand Marcos in Philippine presidential election.

1987—Iraqi missile rips the U.S. frigate *Stark* in the Persian Gulf, killing thirty-seven American sailors. Congress holds hearings to investigate sale of U.S. arms to Iran to finance Nicaraguan *contra* movement.

1988—George Bush is elected president. President Reagan and Soviet leader Gorbachev sign INF treaty, eliminating intermediate nuclear forces. Severe drought sweeps the United States.

Index

Page numbers in boldface type indicate illustrations.

About the Author

Jim Hargrove has worked as a writer and editor for more than ten years. After serving as
an editorial director for three Chicago area publishers, he began a career as an independent
writer. He has contributed to works by nearly twenty different publishers. His Childrens
Press titles include biographies of Mark Twain, Steven Spielberg, Abraham Lincoln, Martin
Van Buren, Harry Truman, Dwight D. Eisenhower, Lyndon B. Johnson, and Richard Nixon.
With his wife and daughter, he lives in a small Illinois town near the Wisconsin border.